How to choose a Franchise

Practical Tips from a Top Franchise Broker

By Daniel Brunell

President of Dearborn West, LLC
Franchise Development

www.DearbornWest.com

Greenstill Press

Printed in the United States of America

Table of Contents

Forward

I have been in the recruiting field for over thirty years, and I have spent the last several working exclusively in the franchise and business opportunity arena. The potential for growth is almost limitless due to a massive shift in how people look at making a living.

Just a generation ago most young people joined the working world with hopes of finding a long term job with a good company that could offer them a future. This is a concept that seems incredible by today's standards. In the 21st century, young people do not expect to have one job anymore than they expect to own one car in their lifetimes. In fact, more young people than ever are turning to business ownership as the preferred career path.

A clear indication of this trend toward entrepreneurialism however, can be witnessed by observing our higher education system. According to a study by the Ewing Marion Kaufman Foundation, in 1980 there were fewer than 300 Universities in the United States that offered course work in entrepreneurship. By 2007 there were more than 2400 Universities teaching entrepreneurship and now, almost every school offering a business major does. Many are now even offering advanced degree programs for entrepreneurs.

This explosive growth is clearly due to the demand in the marketplace and has helped fuel the self employment surge. There is an enthusiasm for self employment never before seen in the post industrial age. Many factors are driving this trend, but chief among them is globalization. In the scope of about a generation, we have entered into a truly global economy. The interdependence between nations is now so great that one major player's recession can trigger economic turmoil across the globe.

The globalization of the economy has created an intensely competitive business environment. As companies strive to reduce costs and become more efficient, farming out certain components of their business makes sense. Most companies used to produce in house, all of the components that went into their finished product. Now parts are typically made by suppliers. In many cases, final assembly is outsourced as well. Additionally, companies used to perform all of the functional roles necessary to run their operations in house. This is no longer the case either.

The outsourcing of production and business processes has resulted in the fracturing of the traditional corporate structure. This has created a pyramid of interdependent relationships. At the top of the pyramid you have a client company that is integrating services from vendors who provide outsourced solutions for a multitude of business functions. In turn, each of the vendors is also a client company with various other vendor companies supporting their efforts. This fracturing has caused a shrinking number of jobs in major corporations, but it has created immense opportunities for entrepreneurs to provide the services that were once generated in house. The demand for these supplier companies is one of the key drivers of the new age of entrepreneurialism.

Another key driver specifically in the United States, has been the deterioration of the business friendly environment for major corporations. The U.S was once the most desirable place in the world for corporate headquarters. The rule of law, respect for property rights and reasonable taxation were bedrock principles in post World War II America. Unfortunately, government overreach and punitive taxes made the US much less attractive for many years. Fortunately, recent rollbacks of taxes and regulations has created a vibrant economy, and once again the US is a top location to do business.

The value of self determination has long been core to the American spirit and once again it is driving people to seek new frontiers of opportunity. This time the frontiers are in the business world instead of the prairies and plains of a sparsely populated continent, but they hold just as much promise.

Chapter One - Why be self employed?

It's helpful to have a clear vision of why, before we can truly grasp how. We need to examine our individual reasons for being self employed in the first place, so that our appreciation of the stakes is crystal clear. Simply wanting our own business is not enough. We need to define the specific end result that we want to achieve by owning a business. This exercise makes it very clear to us why we should give the business our all.

Very few people make a living pursuing their passion in life. Some people get to live their dream and make great money doing it, but they are unique. Most business owners are not trying to revolutionize and industry. They don't want to change the world or be the next Steve Jobs. They just want to be able to make a living on their own terms and not be dependent on an employer for their daily bread. In other words, they want freedom, not fame.

For most of us, our career is a vehicle that allows us to gain access to the things in life that are truly important. Any business can have its frustrations, but they need to be taken in the right context. If you have a clear vision of what your business can help you achieve for yourself or your family, it minimizes the impact of the parts of the business you may not enjoy as much. After all, what element of business isn't worth enduring in order to reach your goals? As long as what you do is legal, moral and ethical, there are no obstacles that aren't worth overcoming in pursuit of your desired outcome. So we need to determine what our specific goals are and in order to do so, we should think back to what motivated us in the first place.

Your motivating factor might be a desire for more time with your family, better control of your destiny, more money or pursuing a specific passion. You should identify whatever the primary driver is for you and then flesh out the accompanying goals that go along with it. Let's assume you want to own your business so you can have control of your time and be a better father/mother/husband/wife. If you sketched out the specific objectives that went along with that it might look like this:

- Be involved in my kids lives on a daily basis

- Make sure my kids get the best possible education

- Spend more time with my significant other

- Interact more with my extended family and friends

- Give back to my community

- Continue to make a good living

- Pursue my own personal enrichment goals

These are the kind of things that will drive you every day. By keeping these goals in front of you and enjoying the benefits that come with attaining them, you will not only be able to suffer the slings and arrows inherent in business ownership, you will actually *enjoy* the opportunity to face them! Additionally, knowing what you want your life to look like will enable you to find a business opportunity that will support those objectives instead of making you compromise them.

Chapter Two - Why buy a franchise?

In the course of my business, I am often asked "When I buy a franchise, what do I get for my money?" The short answer is "a business model." A business model is a framework for creating economic value, in other words, it's a system for making money. A tool, essentially.

Many first time owners confuse the investment in a franchise as a purchase of physical property, when what a franchise represents is intellectual property. The capital equipment, inventory, furnishings, fixtures, buildout costs, etc. are part of a business whether it is franchised or not. The real value in a franchise is that you get a fully formed, proven business model. An effective business model is the difference between success and failure in a business.

The old maxim that most businesses fail because they are undercapitalized is false. Most of these businesses wouldn't have been considered undercapitalized if they would have had an adequate business plan. Every year thousands of well capitalized startups with brilliant ideas for a product or service fail. This is not for lack of money, it is because they eventually burn up all of their cash while trying to develop a system for delivering their product into the hands of a paying customer. All business models are initially perfected by trial and error. This is a very costly process that most small businesses cannot afford to live through. That is why so many private startups fail where franchises succeed.

The costs associated with perfecting a business model will almost always eclipse the cost of paying a franchise fee. The average franchise fee is about 30k. Most starts up waste more than that in advertising costs alone, while they experiment with different marketing strategies. The advantages of having the learning and cost curves reduced to a fraction of the "learn as you go" method, are very significant to say the least.

The other cost component of a franchise is the royalty. This is a fee paid for on-going support which of course includes continuous improvement of the business model, access to vendor discounts, product R&D, marketing and advertising programs, etc. Typical support royalties are between 6% and 8% of revenue. This fee usually pays for itself due to the savings realized when the franchisee purchases goods and services for the business at below market, national account rates. Additionally, most franchisees will experience much higher sales than they would as a private company – greatly in excess of 8% higher - because of the franchisor's well designed marketing strategy.

A franchise may not be right for everyone and they are certainly not all created equal, but a good business model can lower the risk factor and accelerate one's potential for long term success. As always, the key is finding the right match between the model and the operator.

Chapter Three - Is it easier to buy an existing business?

You might think so, but it can be far more problematic than a startup. The biggest issue for me, is that there are thousands of fully formed, excellent business models that typically cost less to develop and offer a tremendous amount of choice for potential owners. If you want to be a business owner, but you limit yourself to only considering the businesses that you can find for sale locally, you are missing out on 80% of the market. It is like going to an apple orchard and insisting that you will only take apples that are already on the ground.

Acquiring an existing business seems like a logical route to pursue, but often it is not the best way to go for your first business. The primary reason for this is a lack of business ownership experience. There is a big difference between managing a large business and owning a small business. As a vice president for a Fortune 500 company and later a Chief Operating Officer of a mid-sized company, I had considerable business experience prior to becoming a business owner. However, like a lot of former executives, I really wasn't ready for all of the unknowns associated with running a small business. No longer do you have the support staff that took care of all of the functional roles such as accounting and finance or human resources, real estate, legal etc.

Standing in line to get permits and dealing with phone or utility company representatives can be frustrating, but not knowing what things need to be addressed, is what can create big trouble for your new business. When buying an existing business, it might be best for first timers to buy a franchised business. This way the books will likely be clean and you will have access to training from the corporate staff, who know how to teach you to run the model the way it was designed to work.

The other reason why an acquisition may not be viable simply comes down to access. The way that most people go about looking for an existing business is by looking through broker listings posted on various websites. This is a logical approach, but unfortunately what it yields most often is nothing more than frustration. The reality is that the best businesses are rarely listed with a broker. They are typically sold to a family member, an employee, a competitor or a friend of the business owner. In other words, there are already people waiting to purchase the business before the owner is ready to sell it. When the owner is ready he simply goes to the people he knows and offers it up and if one of them wants it, he has his lawyer process the transaction and it is a done deal before the general public ever knows it was for sale.

Unfortunately, many of the businesses listed at broker sites have some inherent flaws associated with them. In any case, none of the owners friends, family, employees or competitors were interested in buying his business, so what does that tell you? Quite often the business is just simply overpriced, but many times there are bigger problems that may prove difficult for the new owner to overcome. Things like a bad image can be fixed, but a bad location can only be fixed by moving, which can be costly. If you want to buy an existing business it is often going to be a "fixer upper," so you should have experience in turning around flagging profit centers and be ready to spend the time and money required to do so.

Alternatively, if you wish to find a good quality resale try some old fashioned networking. Business owners know other business owners and they can help you with introductions. Poke around at the local chamber of commerce or the Rotary Club. Talk to as many local business owners as possible and ask them who they know that might be ready to sell. The best source of high quality businesses that might be good targets for acquisition will be the CPAs in your market. These folks keep the books and do the taxes for the local business community and they will know if their clients are ready to sell, so don't forget to talk to them too.

Chapter Four - How much does it cost to start a franchise?

The total investment for developing a franchise can range from a few thousand dollars for a simple home based business to several million for a hotel. The total investment represents the costs of the franchise fee, furnishings, fixtures and equipment, inventory, site improvements, permits, professional fees, initial marketing and any other costs directly related to opening your business. On top of this, the capital required to fund the initial operations of the business can add several thousand additional dollars per month until the cash flow breakeven point is achieved.

Each franchise company has qualifying financial criteria that generally considers the net worth, and/or liquidity of the potential franchisee. The requirements vary from company to company, but they serve as a rough gauge as to whether the candidate has the financial wherewithal to successfully start one of their outlets.

The basic rule of thumb is that you will need approximately 30% of the total investment in liquid funds and you can finance the remaining 70% (provided you have assets such as savings or home equity that exceed the amount you wish to borrow). Generally, the total investment figure does not include much working capital. The total of your budgeted monthly operating expenses combined with your personal living expenses for about a year is what you will need to have set aside in addition to the 30% in liquid funds.

The second biggest reason businesses fail is because they are undercapitalized, so it is crucial that you have a good cash reserve or other streams of income until your business becomes profitable. Most reputable franchise companies will not grant a franchise to someone that is not clearly qualified, so if close scrutiny of your financial background is not required, this should be a red flag about the franchisor.

When franchise shopping, it is important to look in a price range that is appropriate to your resources. Everyone has different levels of risk tolerance and some people have a working spouse that can cover their personal living expenses while the new business is getting started. It is usually a good idea not to invest more than half of your net worth into a new business venture.

If it sounds like it takes a lot of money, it certainly can, but the number of choices is vast and there are opportunities in most price ranges. The benefits of being a successful franchise owner can be substantial and purchasing a franchise is an excellent way to start a business. Just be sure to stay in your price range and do not overextend your capabilities. Remember, your first business doesn't have to be your last business. If you don't get overextended and you do it right, you will have cash flow and or equity that you can use later to develop bigger and better businesses down the road.

Chapter Five - Where do I find the best opportunities?

Knowing what you should be looking for and what to avoid is an important starting point. As a franchisee recruiter, I am often asked "What is the hot franchise?" This is an honest question, but I can never answer it without adding a disclaimer statement. The designation of being "hot" is a dubious honor at best.

What is considered hot is usually determined by media outlets that are trying to fill space around their advertising. While their writers may have the intent of providing good information, they want to have sensational stories to tell. Often these stories can make something out of nothing or overlook serious red flags. The industry press is often impressed by the number of franchise units the franchisor is selling. What you should ask is "What is the average unit volume that those franchised units are producing?" Then look at the net profits that are being generated at the operating unit level. Who cares if the parent franchisor is making money if the operating units are not? The resale market is littered with businesses formerly considered hot, that did not live up to the expectations of the original franchisees.

The truth is that if something is considered hot, it is most likely either too early, or too late for it to make sense for most investors. It may be too early to get into a hot franchise if it has opened too few locations, or if it has less than three years of operating history. Anything this new is unproven and it will take a big leap of faith for the prospective franchisee. Conversely, it may be too late due to a lack of territory availability or the buy in may already have risen so high that it no longer makes financial sense.

The real question is not, what is the best or hottest franchise, but what franchise will be best for me? This of course is only answerable after a careful examination of your unique skills and objectives (see Chapter Eight). When you buy into a franchise system, the value is not in it being the newest or the best known brand. The real value is in the system for doing business and its ability to be replicated in your location. If you look to what is currently considered hot, you run the risk of owning a business that will be a liability a year or two down the road.

Buying into a franchise system is a lot like investing in a stock. Up and coming franchises are typically the best bet for prospective franchisees. Often, the best time to get into a franchise is when there are between 50 and 200 locations. By the time a franchise has been successfully replicated in 50 locations and can show a positive track record that spans at least three years, you can reasonably assume that they are doing some things right and that you can repeat their success in your market too. Also, at this stage of a franchise company's development, they have built and refined their vendor relationships, have well established franchisee training and support systems, and they know how to launch new businesses properly. Also, they have a vested interest in the success of each and every operating unit, so they will commit the resources necessary to help their franchisees succeed.

So where does one find these up and comers? Well, most people will use the internet to shop for a business opportunity. This is a reasonable method for gathering information and there are many franchise information portals at your disposal, but be careful not to let these define your entire range of options. This is a common mistake and it is easy to get caught in that trap. Not all franchises and business opportunities are created equal and their success is always predicated on having the right fit between the model and the franchisee. When looking for a business, there is no substitute for talking to people. With franchises, having two way discussions with the franchisors and franchisees is imperative to understanding the relative virtues of a given model, but also your fitness for operating it.

Your mission is not to determine the potential viability of the model, if they have multiple successful locations, that has already been established. The question is "Are you cut out to operate the model effectively?" This requires conversations with people who know the model best, such as the current franchisees. It also requires keeping an open mind and trying things other than the internet to source opportunities. Franchisee recruiters, business brokers, franchise owners, industry analysts, potential consumers, CPAs, etc. are all great people to discuss the potential of certain businesses with. Just remember, there is no more valuable source when evaluating a business model, than the people who operate it. So talk to professionals to find the hidden opportunities, but talk to operators to understand the value of the model in real terms.

Remember that a growing franchise with a brand name that is mostly unknown in your market, often represents the best opportunity. As long as the model has been successfully replicated in other markets multiple times and has experienced leadership, it should be a good bet. If you are not sure, visit www.dearbornwest.com and ask for a free consultation.

The Web is a great resource, but whatever you do in your search, be sure to talk to lots of people. You can only gain the subjective information that will make a difference to you personally by speaking with people who operate the franchise units.

Chapter Six - Brand name or brand new?

I am often asked if joining a franchise system with a big brand name is better than pursuing an up and coming concept. The answer is of course, maybe and maybe not. A well developed brand can help bring customers to your new business and shorten your journey to the cash flow breakeven point. But they can also be hard to come by. Many big name franchise brands are no longer attainable for the average aspiring business owner. As a franchise grows and builds on its success, often the bar is raised regarding financial and experience qualifications. This is why the majority of the units of the most recognizable food franchises are owned by large restaurant groups. They have the experience, infrastructure, and financial wherewithal to launch and manage these mega concepts. Additionally, the very reason that people become aware of a particular brand is because someone has purchased the franchise rights in that geography and has developed the brand locally. This can mean that the most desirable territory is no longer available by the time a concept has strong brand identity in a market area.

McDonald's and Taco Bell were once local shops in San Bernardino, California. These giants, like all companies, started off with an unknown brand. The key to the success of a franchise lies not only in having a good product or service, but in having a proven system for doing business that can be replicated. A big part of that system for doing business is having solid sales and marketing programs to build a brand name in your market.

Typically, you will be contractually obligated to spend between 2% and 4% of your revenue on brand building whether the company you choose is a household name or a new comer, so don't plan on saving money on advertising if you go with an established brand.

A newer concept just might be the best choice for a prospective franchise operator. You may be able to get in early on a future mega brand, but more importantly you may find a company that has a great stake in your success and will bend over backward to help you. You may also be able to meet an underserved need in the marketplace and build equity in your business more quickly. Also, newer concepts are often more agile and can respond to market needs more readily.

When looking at an up and coming franchise, it is important to look for franchising experience among the members of the management team. Also, try to find a company that has at least twenty units and 3 to 5 years of operating success. These minimum criteria can help you determine if a concept is going to have legs in your area too. Whether a big brand name or an up and comer is right for you depends on your unique situation, but either way, finding a solid business model should be your primary objective.

Chapter Seven - What is a Biz Op?

A licensed business opportunity or "biz op" is similar to a franchise in that it is a fully formed business model. It is a complete system for doing business that typically offers everything from start up assistance, to all of the necessary processes, equipment, sales and marketing tools and complete training. The core difference is that in a franchise, you are essentially going into partnership with the franchisor. They will have tremendous sway over how, and what you may do with your business. They will also share in your proceeds. In a licensed model, there are essentially no royalties and no rules. You are buying their business model, training and startup assistance. You will belong to their fraternity of owners, so you can collaborate, enjoy group purchasing power and maybe enjoy ongoing support, but you are 100% in control of your business.

The technical difference is regulatory, in that a franchise is required by the Federal Trade Commission to offer a Franchise Disclosure Document to all prospective buyers. The FDD contains twenty-three specific points that explain all of the costs, what they get for their investment and thoroughly defines the relationship. The best biz ops usually offer an equivalent to this document, but are not required to do so. One of the biggest challenges with a biz op is that unlike a franchise, they are not required to provide the name and phone number of every single person who is operating their business model or indicate how many of them have failed. This generally puts more of the burden for due diligence on the buyer, in contrast to the very well defined discovery process most franchisors offer.

For some entrepreneurs the biz op arrangement is ideal. They feel more comfortable being on their own after the start up phase, but they can still reduce their risk and enjoy the benefits of an already perfected system for generating profit. Certain types of businesses are better suited for franchises such as retail stores or restaurants where you need the collective buying power of a large organization or you can benefit from national branding. However, many other businesses do better as a biz op (i.e., dry cleaners and mailbox stores) because the long term value of being in the group may not justify the on-going royalties.

Either way, franchises and Biz Ops can both be an excellent way to get into a lucrative and rewarding business. There are of course, very good and not so good opportunities, irrespective of the structure. Your best bet, as always, is to examine your goals and your own preferences in order to decide which vehicle is right for you.

Chapter Eight - How do I know which model is best for me?

Most people go about answering this question by thinking about the product or service that the business will offer first. Another popular approach is to consider unmet needs in the marketplace that they could address with a new business. Both of these are logical approaches, but unless you want your life to revolve around your business, it is far better to consider your lifestyle objectives first. The greatest thing about starting your own business is that you can structure your lifestyle according to your own preferences instead of someone else's.

Each type of business will have specific implications on your day to day life. Owning a restaurant for instance will give you a very different work week than owning a business consulting firm or a cleaning service. If you really enjoy playing golf, you may think owning a golf store would be ideal, but a retail store owner's work schedule may not be conducive to playing much golf. Your town may be in need of a bagel shop and that type of business could do well, but do you want to get up at 4 am every day? These tend to be the things that will make or break a business for the owner. In order to most effectively choose which business is right for you, it is useful to explore why you want your own business. What are your motivating factors and what do you wish to accomplish through business ownership?

- Is your goal to make more money?

- Are you trying to have better control of your time?

- Are you looking to achieve a better life work balance?

- Do you wish to pursue a particular passion?

- Are you trying to build something that will accumulate equity or just generate a paycheck?

The next step is to determine how you want your work life to flow. Consider things such as when, where and how much you want to work. Then consider what environment will suit you best (i.e., retail, office, industrial, mobile or home based). Once these considerations are identified, then you can determine which business model will support the type of lifestyle you desire. If your first consideration is about the product or service you will offer, then you may need to structure your life to accommodate the business instead of creating a business that gives you access to the life you want.

Chapter Nine - What type of advisors should I have?

There are many advantages to getting help from a professional who knows the inside workings of an industry or issue. Just having someone who can help interpret the jargon associated with a topic that is new to you can be a tremendous help. Most people wouldn't go to court without a lawyer or purchase a home without the help of a realtor.

Top executives in the corporate world typically do not directly approach an employer. They are sought out by an executive recruiter, who evaluates their potential and then introduces them at a high level to the appropriate companies. It doesn't cost the executive anything because the recruiter is paid by the company for finding the right business talent for their organization. The same is now true in the franchise world and working with a competent recruiter is essential to a comprehensive business opportunity search.

When getting into any new endeavor, the problem is not finding answers; it is knowing what questions to ask. Answers are easy to come by, but if you are not sure of all of the relevant questions to ask yourself and others, you are in jeopardy of making mistakes. A franchisee recruiter can help you crystallize your business and lifestyle objectives and then identify opportunities that are closely aligned with your talents, interests and goals. Of course you can also do this yourself, but you could be very diligent in your efforts and still miss out on key opportunities that would be perfect for your unique needs. Like the best career opportunities, the best business opportunities are not typically, widely advertised.

There are thousands of franchises and several times as many biz ops available in North America. A franchisee recruiter can help you sort out the differences between the types of opportunities, so you can determine which format is right for you. Whether it is a franchise or biz op, there are many terrific choices and invariably there are some bad ones. A recruiter can help you locate businesses that meet fundamental quality standards and also help you avoid making a potentially big mistake. Recruiters may not have current agreements with every franchise, but they can often obtain the listing if it meets your requirements as well as their own standards. A key advantage is that the agreements they do have, are generally with proven as well as solid, up and coming or established concepts that will meet the requirements of the new franchise buyer.

One of the biggest challenges for franchise companies is finding entrepreneurs who will be a good fit for their particular business model. As you can imagine, franchisors get thousands of requests for their information packets, but most of these come from people who are not qualified or motivated to actually become a part of their organization. These companies generally cannot support the amount of staff necessary to do an effective job of bringing in new franchisees. This is why the value of a recruiter referred candidate is so significant.

The company is being introduced to a pre-screened individual who meets the basic requirements, understands franchising, is informed about the opportunity and is more than just casually interested. This saves the franchisor a great deal of time and money, so they pay a fee to the recruiter if the candidate becomes a franchisee. This creates a winning scenario for all parties involved. Remember, the purpose of the franchise fee is not to be a profit center for the franchisor. The franchise fee was designed to cover the costs associated with acquiring and training new franchisees.

In the final analysis, the choice and the responsibility for researching the opportunity are yours, but as you contemplate such a huge decision, you should not leave any stones unturned. Getting help from a competent recruiter is one of the best resources you can employ and since the seller pays the fee, the service is free to you.

Additionally, you will want to have a competent franchise attorney review the Franchise Disclosure Document (FDD) and franchise agreement before you sign on the bottom line. It is imperative that you utilize an attorney who specializes in this area. Otherwise you will have someone who will likely kill your deal and run up a large legal bill while he is learning franchise law. The simple fact is that while there are typically some finer points that can be negotiated; there is not a lot of wiggle room in these contracts. This is because the franchisor is legally obligated to disclose any material changes to the agreement in the Franchise Disclosure Document. The entire concept of franchising is based on uniformity, so having separate agreements that are all over the map is counterproductive. The role of the attorney is vital, but it is more about telling you what you are saying yes to than it is about rewriting the agreement. A competent attorney will know this before you start.

If you have a CPA as part of your financial life, by all means you should discuss your plans to buy a franchise with them, but typically you don't need to go out and hire one to review a new franchise opportunity for you. Accounting is a forensic art and accountants are experts at identifying what happened and how to make the most of it, but not necessarily great at looking at the potential of a brand new opportunity. If you are doing an acquisition where there is history and numbers to evaluate, absolutely bring an accountant in to review the P&Ls if you do not have expertise in this area.

However, if you are looking at starting a new franchise location, your best bet is to talk to as many franchisees within the franchisor as possible. Look for franchisees that operate in areas that are demographically similar to your own. Ask them thorough questions about revenue and operating expenses. These locations will provide the most likely indicator as to what your potential might be. The franchisor will likely equip you with tools to be able to make reasonable projections that you can incorporate into your business plan.

Another key advisor to tap into is a lender of some kind. Doing this early in the process is vital. Especially if this is your first business, it can be really hard to figure out what investment level you can truly afford. Every franchise has a minimum net worth requirement. Some companies are more concerned with liquidity than assets, but this assures the franchisor that you will have the appropriate resources necessary to operate one or more of their units. A good lender can help you establish your potential for borrowing. Knowing what investment range will work best will save you from wasting tremendous amounts of time looking at the wrong opportunities. Whether you utilize a 401k conversion outfit, an SBA lender or some other source, getting a good handle on your finances should be your first step.

Clearly there are many advisors you can involve on the professional side and a good recruiter can help refer you to competent people in all of these areas. Keep in mind though that an effective business search is all about talking to people and you should take a 360 degree approach. Talk to people on all sides of the potential business, even people who you think might be customers of such a business. Also, talk to your family and friends, as they can be very important advisors. Just keep in mind that most people are not cut out to own a business, so you need to filter the opinions that you gather and weigh them properly. Successful entrepreneurs all share a common thread and that is that they see opportunities where other people see roadblocks. Don't let someone's negativity be a roadblock for you in the pursuit of your goals. Use the information you gather to make you think – not to stop your progress.

Chapter Ten - What is next?

FUD is an acronym used in sales and marketing circles. It stands for Fear, Uncertainty and Doubt. Marketers sometimes try to trigger these emotions in order to motivate you to utilize their product or service. These feelings are not hard to trigger because they are naturally occurring and most people experience some level of each when faced with a major decision. Buying a franchise or licensed business opportunity can cause plenty of FUD and it should – buying into the wrong opportunity can be hazardous to your life savings. Remember, the choice is not "What is the best franchise to buy?" – It is "Which franchise is right for my personal needs?" Many people learn the hard way. I hear over and over from people that they wish they had known me before they bought their first franchise, because I could have saved them a lot of trouble (and money).

My company connects people with business opportunities throughout North America. The franchise companies pay us fees to perform this service, so our help is free. Starting a business is a big deal, so don't go it alone. We can quickly and painlessly help you narrow your search and find options that suit your unique needs. You are never obligated to invest in any opportunity until the seller decides they want to formally offer one to you and you are positive you want to accept that offer, so there is no pressure.

You certainly can find something on your own, but we can help you find things that you would otherwise miss. Visit www.dearbornwest.com today to schedule a simple conversation about your potential. Our fees are always paid by the seller, so you get our world class experience at no cost. It pays to know someone. Get to know us.

About the Author

Dan Brunell is President of Dearborn West, LLC, a national consulting firm providing franchisee and licensee recruiting services to hundreds of leading companies worldwide. He can be reached at dbrunell@dearbornwest.com.